MANDORLA

OTHER BOOKS BY
NANCY HOLMES

The Adultery Poems
(Ronsdale, 2002)

Down to the Golden Chersonese: Victorian Lady Travellers
(Sono Nis, 1991)

Valancy and the New World
(Kalamalka, 1988)

Mandorla

POETRY BY

Nancy Holmes

RONSDALE PRESS

RONSDALE PRESS
3350 West 21st Avenue
Vancouver, B.C., Canada V6S 1G7
www.ronsdalepress.com

Typesetting: Julie Cochrane, in New Baskerville 11 pt on 13.5
Cover Design: Julie Cochrane
Cover Photo: *The Virgin of Vladimir,* an early twelfth-century icon, egg tempera on wood
Paper: Ancient Forest Friendly Rolland "Enviro" — 100% post-consumer waste, totally chlorine-free and acid-free

Ronsdale Press wishes to thank the Canada Council for the Arts, the Government of Canada through the Book Publishing Industry Development Program (BPIDP), and the Province of British Columbia through the British Columbia Arts Council for their support of its publishing program.

Library and Archives Canada Cataloguing in Publication

Holmes, Nancy, 1959–
Mandorla / Nancy Holmes.

Poems.
ISBN 1-55380-029-X

I. Title.

PS8565.O637M35 2005 C811'.54 C2005-903525-0

At Ronsdale Press we are committed to protecting the environment. To this end we are working with Markets Initiative (www.oldgrowthfree.com) and printers to phase out our use of paper produced from ancient forests. This book is one step towards that goal.

Printed in Canada by Marquis, Quebec

For Doug, Ian and Alex,

and for everyone who's been good

to us over the years,

especially Mom, Dave, Jill, Sylvia, Jo,

Linda, Holli and Sue

CONTENTS

ICONOGRAPHY

SHACKLE OF GOLD

ACKNOWLEDGEMENTS

I'd like to thank the Leighton Colony at the Banff Centre and the B.C. Ministry of Culture, Small Business and Tourism for providing me with space and time to begin to write many of the poems in this book. Thanks to Karen Connelly who read earlier versions of this manuscript and to Ronald Hatch my editor and publisher.

I am also grateful for the support of the editors of the small literary journals and anthologies who first published many of these poems or versions of them: *CV2, Grain, The Road Home, Event, Windsor Review, Dandelion, Dalhousie Review, Malahat Review, Prairie Fire, Fiddlehead, Brobdingnagian Times* (Ireland), *New Quarterly, Tower, Kaleidoscope, Who Lies Beautifully: The Kalamalka Anthology, Rideau River Press Broadside for the Tree Reading Series, Room of One's Own, Corkboard, Echolocation, Grey Borders.*

mandorla — [< Italian *mandorla* almond (c. 1288), almond-shaped ornamental motif (c. 1367) < post-classical Latin *amandola* ALMOND *n.*]

An almond-shaped panel or decorative space, usually framing an image of Christ.

— *Oxford English Dictionary*

ICONOGRAPHY

The icons of the Eastern Orthodox church often present the Virgin in poses that have particular significance. Many of the following poems are titled with the name of one of those hieratic poses. Some of the images referred to in these poems come from the Byzantine museum in Athens and the deserted Byzantine town of Mistra in Greece. Others were gleaned from various books about Byzantine art and Russian icons.

Early Versions

i.

She travelled from the east,
scavenging along the Silk Road,
shadowing caravans.

With her ripe slanted eyes,
she was looking for love,
the nomad's lesson, the Arab lesson,

the whole lesson.

In a bazaar, she met a painter.
The Turkish coffee was strong,
the noise of buying and selling
operatic.

She sat by his side on the street.
He crushed
lapis lazuli into paste,
mashed berries, stone and bark
into gritty red cream.

Later, he showed her his secret
hoard of gold foil.
Attention puffed up her puny banner of pride
and she lay down with him.

While she slept, he peeled
the delicate golden
membranes from her eyes

then slipped away, leaving only
a bowl of roses
between her thighs.

ii.

She's huddled behind the flower stalls,
her eyes naked and trembling.

Before God gets her,
let us give her some advice:

> *Sleep will never come,*
> *so you may as well get up.*
>
> *Wear blue; it never hurts.*
>
> *Often it is best simply to*
> *cover your head and ears*
> *with a good thick cloth.*
>
> *You may as well toss out*
> *those bracelets and earrings.*
>
> *Where you are going,*
> *you won't need*
> *handcuffs or bells.*
>
> *And while you can, use*
> *that cosmic cosmetic:*
>
> *chalk those tragic eyes*
> *with kohl.*

iii.

Still, tears will come,
and sand will sting,
so where is the relief?

Try this recipe for sore eyes:

> Pluck two petals from an Asiatic lily,
> flimsy as rice paper
> but scented and spicy.
>
> Dip the petals in rose water.
> Press each — limp and dripping —
> against a boiling eyeball.
>
> Let them rest there,
> until they wrinkle,
>
> grow stiff,
>
> become thoroughly
> salted and dried.

Annunciation

(mosaic, British Museum)

Finding the rupture
in something she thought whole

is the lesson she learns the hard way,
by going in

to true exile: brick wall and orchard.
Inside, the elegant Byzantine arch discloses

a glistening marble alcove, an empty bench.
But the original fault lies

wedged between bone, between
the plates of the skull that float on the brain

where a fingertip can dent the tissue
as it can an apple's flesh.

To be born is to be broken.

No one is whole.

The fruit falls from the tree
and lands on its own bruise.

Platyera

(the child appears in a circular medallion
over the Virgin's breast and womb)

i.

The church's walls are rinsed
with fresco and fresh mosaic.
As she walks corridors,
she presses soft putty
and crayoned walls.

Alone in the courtyard, she holds
her hands up to the light.
Her fingertips glow red and gold
like cut-open
pennies. Her rosy hands begin
to hum with hope,
her temples fill
with bells and bright
blue birds.

Her body is
a sunbathed dome:

white cells swollen with solution,
overlapping joints
of hot red tile.

ii.

But this is the truth about
incarnation:

her body is a dream home
God won at the fair.
Her own fingers have sold
Him the lucky ticket.

She wants to buy it back
but God loves the floor plan.
He can hardly wait
to move in.

He runs around like a kid
pushing all the buttons.
He jabs the pouch
of slippery bones
and pounds on walls.

Could He knock a door
through here? He pokes and prods
her marble belly.

How about a pantry
or kitchen island?

But a butcher block
for sure.

Nativity

(fresco in the Church of the Peribleptos, Mistra)

the wound is opened to air
but none comes out

her body is rubble and bruises
God has picked through her flesh
bent her bird-thin bones
out of the way

the halo hurts her eyes
like rubies her nipples cut
through her skin

now the midwife unwinds
and winds the glistening cloth

where is he?
where is he who is
everything new?

burnt by the light
he lies wrinkled
in the barnyard straw
his fists still bloody
and shredded

he tried to hang on
to every organ in her body
as he slid out

as if she were the rope

and not the well

Blacherniotissa

(The Virgin holds the child in both hands)

she stays in the alcove with the child
now that she is devoted to fear

fear of moving at the wrong moment
fear of dropping
fear of slapping
fear of pinching
fear of temper
fear of slipping
fear of pins and nails
fear of noises that make his body splay
                                        like a jumping cat
fear of a grip too tight
fear of a mind too
wandering fear of being
empty and wrung out

and every night
her fingers are boneless rags
unable to wipe up the screams of the crying child

one morning she finds
she cannot reach her heart

it has fallen from its hook
onto the marble floor
spidery veins
twitch at the feet of the sobbing child

he stops crying
picks up the stringy heart
drops it

picks it up again

starts smiling
looks up at her

drops it

waits for her to laugh
or leap

Mandorla

(a halo surrounds the whole bodies of mother and child)

look
through
this keyhole
shaped like an almond
so you too can see them:
the mother and child asleep
in the sun that saintly streams
through the rose and pearl glass
her lemony curls blanket the floor
the baby woven into the warm fibre
the heart shuttling over the loom's
braided span of sun, lock, hand,
each succulent breath
freshly milked and
honeyed — can it
be they are
lambs
to the

lambs to the
no
no cruel word can enter here

Hodegetria

(the Virgin holds the child in her left arm,
her right arm indicating the child: "showing the Way")

As they walk by the great estate,
they see a crew of angels working,
tuning the harp of the grass,
edging, fertilizing,
brandishing fiery shears,
and digging a deep hole.

Good old boys, all of them,
their white overalls,
their angelic joshing.

The child stops at the gate.
The angels wave, tease the child
with the lawn's green tilt.

"Let's go," she says.
She hates this place,
the ornate mansion, all the trappings
of God's power.
Each Sunday, He rides His mower
around the garden,
or swaggers down the driveway
zapping weeds.

The angels get off their knees,
trumpet out: "Come on kid,
Come in.
Whatchya 'fraid of?"

She tries to pull the child away
but the angels swing open the gate.
He wriggles from her grasp and runs
into God's backyard,
onto the forbidden green lawn.

The angels bring out a soccer ball,
swing a bat, chase the boy
as they bounce the ball off his head.

"This way! This way!" she shouts
standing on the sidewalk,
helpless, ignored.

As he turns
and turns, increasingly
bewildered and blinded,
they jostle
him, knock him
with their great padded shoulders,
nudge him towards the black
hole they've been digging.

"Stop! This way!"
she cries, as if she knows the way

the child will fall headfirst
into God's dark plot.

Communion

A garden is a flimsy cage.

Seeds run wild.
Rogue apple trees snap
at the barbed wire.
Weeds vandalize the tidy paths.

And God just can't keep his hands out.
He feeds the garden junk food
through gleaming genetic bars.

Before you know it,
it's not just his fingers.
His appetite's got into the garden, too.
He's scooping up the newly fallen
bodies of the pears.

And once he's had a taste of that ripe treat
he begins to dream of other exquisite dishes:

like the brains and bitter marrow
of the beasts.

Deëis

(The Virgin stands by the crucifixion
with John the Baptist)

His fanatical voice is always with her.

He says she must do it this way.
Even before the child was born
it was ordained.

What did you think you were getting?
he asks. Life is harsh.
God uses tough love on all his children.
But consider the walnut, the root,
your own shelled heart.

So every day she nails her child
onto the golden bus,

the blue bird
O Byzantium!

and at the end of the day
she's busy, so busy,
unpinning
the bloody nails,

unstrapping the child's
broken feet and hands.

The Text

The child was delivered to God all right.
Logos, God sighed,
slitting the school open
like an envelope.

He pulled the child out,
all tender vellum,
unfolded the tiny arms and legs
and began to read.

But whoever wrote the child
had a serious disability.
The child didn't make sense.
The whole script read sideways.
Speech disorder, dyslexia, dysgraphia, apraxia.
You name it.
The handwriting was illegible.

While the child babbled
in God's leather-bound hands,
He decided
This one is too much trouble.

He closed the kid
and shelved him.

This one will never work.

Eleousa

(merciful or tender Virgin, embracing the child —
Virgin of Vladimir)

after a long winter
the Russian churches have been re-gilded
the domes flaunt themselves above brown veils of fog

but the sunlight lasts only a few polluted hours
the museum closes its doors for the night
and the heat is turned down

on the wall she is only a fragment
she is no longer the girl who loved wild figs and red skirts
her face is a tarnished locket
her gypsy eyes
dried olives

her brittle cheek
presses against the child's round head
centuries later still blurred with the down
and dents of birth

the rest of the icon has rotted away

only this shrivelled core
          this preservation
                    this double dandelion globe of gold
remains

Orans

(The Virgin holds open her hands
and arms, no child)

Mother, the mind is a polished chalice.
It nurses a spot of wine
in its bowl
or, empty,
simply mirrors itself.

Mother, I see
you have lost your eyes
to the iconoclasts.
Your body is a battered silver platter,
the holes
the absolution in your thought.

Mother, I tell you and I pray,
and what's there?
Nothing.
You cannot turn
you are so welded
to the wall with God's hot gaze.

Over the centuries, your arms are beaten open.
You tarnish at the wrists.
Your fingers break off one by one.
Your face grows a crust of thick black veils.

Dormition

(death of the Virgin)

her eyes are raisins, leathery relics
shrivelled in a sealed casket

the halo is a rusted plate that once dished up her head
her limbs are dirty nests of swaddling

once she's laid in the dark
roots and worms finally finger open
the ruptured shroud

but, oh the wrenching
long scented hands of her son the gardener
lever her out of the earth
he wipes away the mushy veins
ignores the hoard of black bent metal
around her decaying head
and throws her onto a tray

he turns away
kneels in the dirt
keeps digging

now to her amazement
she has become a peeled bulb
rattling on the wire tray

she is the wet colour of cream
clear as an eyeball, immortal as an onion

visible in her heart
a thin green shoot

SHACKLE OF GOLD

At the turn of the last century, the Mazepas,
a Ukrainian family, immigrated to Canada
and settled in north-east Alberta.
The family had several children, but these poems
are mostly about the three girls, one who married and had
three daughters of her own (one of whom was my mother),
one who had an undefined mental handicap
and who lived several decades in an institution,
and one who never married and who lived her long life in
the original mud-caulked, three-room pioneer home.

What Made Them Leave?

After the village burnt down,
did the pregnant wife collapse in shock?
Did the priest's black
        skirts swish
over her bursting body
as he ran to get the midwife?

Did the child whimper and turn
        from the breast,
blue milk pooling in its mouth?

Was the silent child brought to the new world
on the steamer, bundled in rags and scarves,
left on the deck for hours   unchanged   the mother so sick?
Did the virgin's icon come over with them
        wrapped face down in a wine-red trunk?
Did they notice as they sailed out of the Great War,
        left behind the treaties of Paris?

After ocean and continent, they arrive in a pure white place:
the snow criss-crosses
        the train tracks, the roads, it throws
                icy nets into the air,   over
the destination.
The child's eyes slide over each
        other, knock into each other, trying
to watch the falling
                snow, and
everything on the train   and now

caught in one bare town,
ending a journey
        with that old lullaby   called hope.

The Last Ice Age

the immigrants saw ancient grassland
grassland thatched shut for ten thousand years
and carved it open

riches glistered beneath the shaggy coat

mammoth hunters on a carcass
they fished out shrubs, roots, flint
they obliterated prints of hoof and skin-shod foot
they slit the veins and arteries of animal burrows
skimmed meaty topsoil from its bones

through frost, drought, hail
they worked on even when they had enough
they dug and scalped
they sawed and slaughtered
even as the planet thawed beneath their tools
they butchered on

until the last straw of wild grass
was broken
until they milked
the monstrous glaciers dry

The First House

they led the white-flanked house
into pasture to be fattened

mud dripped from its new-made ribs
cut plaster fleshed the planks

with glossy eyes
the new-made creature looked in wonder
upon the endless lake of grass

all around the delicately planted
feet of the house
poppies opened their beaks
hollyhocks rattled
on their stalks

the house soon grazed between the sloughs
dragged steel teeth
through the grass
and the dirt's closed door

the old blue tent's abandoned

the sky's blown over
its canopy flapping, and stuffing
floating away
in the wind

Cultivation

the old wife is always busy
sometimes she works knee-deep in clouds
banging out featherbeds
but usually she gets down to earth

she rips the topsoil off the granite floor
the fertile rug jumps and squeals in her hands —
insects, worms, wishbones
crumble apart
mice, eggshells, mad birds
shit, knots, roots, infants

she beats the carpet with sticks and brooms
she shakes it out
mud and vermin shower down
at our feet, on our doorsteps

clean it up, you worthless girls,
then you can go to the ball

old mother culture: domestic goddess
our secret friend
and wicked stepmother too

The Crown

the church is a pearl
clipped to the grain's gold throat

the house is as pale and cold
as a tsarina's cheek

in winter, snowy furrows
are tucked up to the door
white and sable fur, a collar

into this luxury, three girls are born:
the jewels and flowers of the family

hands like bouquets, eyes like solitaires,
thoughts like opals

the normal one,
who married and moved on

the one who stayed forever on the farm,
spinster and recluse

and a third who . . .
who was
          well, not quite . . .
                    tap tap
a finger on the head

Mothers and Aunts

in the warm weather the girls are up to their ears
in carnations, dahlias and poppies
pulling raspberries off prickly tongues
snagging their fingers on chicken wire
that holds the sweet peas at bay

but in the fall, mothers and aunts
strap apron shields around their waists

out of the garden
they tear cabbages as big as cows' heads
chop off their roots
and hurl them down the hole in the floor

the girls hold hands, creep near the hole
the trap door propped against the white-washed wall
is hairy and brown as a witch's cheek

they watch their mothers and aunts
go down
and down again
into the cellar
where they wrestle the food, bag the promise
bottles of purple bruises
bodies in burlap sacks

nothing can stop them —
out of the way,
shoo, hiss —
not a spell, not a lost child
nothing can stop them

they drag the whole garden into the ground

First Harvest

curtains of grain blow into
the train's dark rooms

stripped now, the shorn land shivers
rubbed raw
like a bride's smooth cheek
against her husband's stubble

in homes and halls
women brush chaff from their coarse skirts
wrap ropes of hair under kerchiefs
fill tables with sizzling lists of food
pleat oily edges of dumplings, whip cream,
tug strings off beans, baste the garden in vinegar,
keep the youngest girls tied to their brooms
and iceboxes

back at the station
the men,
garlic eaters, Bohunks,
learn English the Anglo-Saxon way
through insult

they huddle in small groups
peel cloves of garlic
with stained thumbnails
pop the naked morsels
into their bearded mouths

they finger coins deep in their pockets
and plot their stubborn acts
against the spring

Mermaids in a Blizzard

fields are oceans of chopped up snow and soil
fragile fences are strung out and gutted in the storm
sheds slowly drown in boiling drifts

in the middle of the dark-dug sea
the family hangs on in their house
three little girls swim deeper into the feather bed
play hide-and-seek in its dreamy billows
float in sheets and downy quilts
feed us breakfast in bed, they giggle
coming up for words
the mother scolds, but
scrolls thin pancakes into minnows
feeds them on the sly
dolphins, lazybones she says
even the silent child laughs

the morning lasts and lasts
the light never changes
the blizzard has blotted out
the foreign land

the mother feeds the burning stove
tiny cat-pink mouths

outside, silver windows weep with slush
inside, they grow thick scales of frost

the daylight is split open
turned inside out
unseen, the king's ruby ring
lands in the sink
and rattles down the drain

the daylight is rinsed clean
scraped boneless
the daylight becomes
a slippery opal fillet
in the cook's cold hands

The War on Drugs, Circa 1930

"destroy those poppies, m'am"

the policeman told the mother
who looked like a dope fiend indeed
a dope fiend in a baba's kerchief
consorting in her den
in vapours of steam from pickling beets

rafters in the shed were stripped
of brittle ribbons and clattering pods
herbs were hauled to the fire pit
and burned

"every boss is crazy!"
the mother and the father grumbled
the children smacked
the fire with sticks
drove clouds of smoke into the air

then into the sky
the sunset staggered
enswathed in bronze and pink
so stoned
it tripped, collapsed on some cushions

and lay there, fanning itself
shamelessly lolling about
for all the world to see

people in town *tsk*-ed, *tsk*-ed
those foreigners! look what happens —
the whole world gone to pot
now something
will have to be done
about the sunset

now that it too
has sunk
so low

Why Their Surname is "Mazepa," the Same as the Revolutionary Hetman and Enemy of the Tsar

Maybe some nobleman went to Europe on a tour
and came back loaded with ideas and furniture.
In a radical fit, the count bestowed the glorious name on a poor serf
with a long nose, a ratty beard, and small blue eyes.

Or an old patriarch, as a joke, named every peasant on the estate
after his besotted son's favourite Byronic hero.
Cackling and illiterate, he spat on the Italian marble,
put the young buck in his place, and ruined for good his love of reading.

Or a twisty-eyed peasant told a drunken bureaucrat
he wanted this daring name. The drunk wrote it down, uncaring,
shouted "Next." The other peasants winked and laughed,
the next one said "St. Nicholas," then "Napoleon," "Peter the Great"

and "Baba Yaga" until the drunken clerk, ink-stained and befuddled,
caused a small riot, became his own Russian story.

The Wedding Skirt

when the girls lifted the lid
of the old trunk
out leapt a fabric hand
red and raw as a granny's claw

at first they screamed
as it laid veiny fringes
along their shoulders
hooked their waists
in a crippling sash

careful now, careful, their mother told them
the wedding skirt will be yours one day

but hardly listening
they were drawn to the whispered
fortune telling

and the skirt's gypsy fair

they romped on the carousel of its swirl
gambled in the blue flash of embroidery
smuggled each other into
the freak show of its folds

all the time
their fortunes dealt and spun
till they were feverish

past and future carnivals
caught them
tossed them

dressed them up
and dressed them down

The Church

the priest's robes are charred and sooty
he wears chains around his neck, charms in his beard
when he walks on snow, he burns black holes

in the house, he opens his travelling case
offers the farmers soap and futures
sells them pin-up Virgins in pink and blue

but when the father and the mother go to town
the lurking priest leads his church across the prairie
brings it to the doorstep of the locked-up house

his holy fingers rap the door
he knocks and halloos

"come out," the priest calls to the children inside
"come out and see the pretty church
come see its ivory horns, its lustrous eyes"

the children huddle in the cellar
with their orders:
do not open the door, let no one in

they hear the church's panting breath
the church's jingling clanging bells
they say nothing, they don't move
until even the most frightened sleep
clutching tear-stained pebbles and each other's hands

the priest hitches the house to the church
the church strains in its harness
hauls the house off its hole
exposing the sleeping children
soft and snotty as shell-less snails

the priest scoops them up

"seeds," he lisps and counts them
"oats," he whispers to the harnessed ox
who moans

Why Was This Story *(That Told Us Tales)* Told?

once *(long ago)*
she was going to marry

(it was early one summer
when the wind braided the tips of wheat
into a silken shawl of apple green)

but her lover drowned in a slough
(choked with weeds,
quilted with treacherous loons)

for days, in the basement of the *(pearl-white, onion-domed)*
church the lover's body was laid out on blocks of ice

(the ice drained slowly into the basket of straw,
his body draining, too, white and hollow)

outside men dug the hole
women baked in the hall
(there was no sound, not a clanking of pans
not the chink of a shovel
they were all ghosts in sympathy)

this is why she never married
why she became a recluse

(even now they look up from their tasks
they set down their spoons, their spades
they want to tell us something else
something more about this story)

but now *(out of their mouths comes a black wind*
that floods the basement, the slough, the summer,
and salts the dismal crop of grain)

red poppies seed themselves
in the creek's green bed
(the nursing calf drains the bottle
and in her lap lays its sacrificial head)

Before She Was Finally Sent Away

the third daughter stayed
indoors all winter outside
the wind sifted the powdered snow

inside a lone geranium leaned against
the frosted pane

the plant was feeble from lack
of light each thin stem
nearly toppled by
a bright red brain

the blooms hurt her
head like blows red fists fell
on her temples
gritty snow bloody petals
the plates of her skull
eggshell and pulp

the father too old to nurse her
climbed around her
hammered an icon of the Virgin
over the bed a benediction
of plaster dust sprinkled down
on her lips
scalp lashes

now both faces are fixed
on white walls
the girl's eyes crushed
in crimson sockets
the Virgin's head
locked in a shackle of gold

The Asylum That is Somewhere

no one is there
but the guard and the nurse

no one knows their names or
where it is

their families died
and others forgot them
or the other way around

around and around
a woman takes words for walks
in her mouth

another felt the gash of her baby's birth
so deeply, all she can do is polish
a tiny skeleton in her head

is there someone groaning?
yes, she is always groaning

and the strange girl of the family
where is she?

a nurse leaves the room
and closes the door

the guard who was standing
sits down

no one knows who pays to keep her
the new children are never told
or taken to see her

when do the payments stop?
or have they stopped?

her history's not there

the end of her natural life
disappeared

Weaning the Baby in the Depression

she kisses its springy skull
milk trickles through the reedy fingers
between the pink gums and the breast
she is the furrow and the rain
sweet and mucky weeks go by

in half a season the gardens come and go
the father shouts, the mother turns away
the baby dragged through sleep
like a ball of dough through flour

the father and the uncles talk of money, more money
the grain stops, falls, lies dead in the dust

the baby's face is powdered with dried milk
the sprouting hair slowly closes the gap in the skull
the infant smiles and dribbles a final drop

the mother opens her dress
removes the baby
plants it in a wooden crib

Lacing Up the Skates

on a winter night instead of language
sails ballooned out of our mouths

our tongues tugged at our breath
until they were rope-burned

our lungs, too, made a canvas escape
launched into the wind
pulling our voices inside out

as we fumbled with the laces of our skates
we began to dread the frozen river:
the dark ice that slid for miles
through the knotted woods

where would our wild rigging
take us?

would we ever be heard from
again?

Snow Angels

that night we could not feel
our own cheeks or each other's hands

our mittens were crusted with miniature balls of snow
that curdled in the tough wool

we ate the crunchy pearls off our mittens
until our tongues grew rough with cuts and edges
like oyster shells

that night we could not see the treacherous ground
blinded by the blaze of Venus in the sky

we slipped on the ice —
crack — sent

spinning
Venus scratching a track across our retinas

crawled over the ice
clawed into a snow bank
blind   sore

prostrate before
the queen of night

who crushed us in her diamond hands
ground us into blood-red cloves

rolled, pinched and hammered us

until here we are:
thorny stars
pinned
to her frozen breast

No Running Water

children's skinny arms pump
pump silver chains out of the earth
chilly links shuffle through their hands
they hold onto rings of the silver bridle
mount and fall off the bucking orange arm
thrown into a whole summer of screaming and
running over sharp stubble and stones
while water gallops into the garden dirt
and later melts mud off new potatoes
tiny globes, eyeballs, cider-clear skin
so thin a thumbnail shaves it
the sensitive young girl shivers
the season swings back in a wide canter
slows, stops, allows the children to comb
its grassy mane and swishing tail
now the long day lowers its thirsty muzzle to a pail
brimming over with mud-fed
          water-peeled
                    summer-simmered flesh

Bigotry

in the kitchen the old man and his wife
play with the budgie at the table
they feed the bird crumbs of cake
show the grandchild its emerald tricks

they have carried their old hatreds far
first there's the Jews, the blacks and the gypsies
coo, coo, they whistle at the bird
that hops over arthritic knuckles

and then there's the new:
those natives get money for nothing
phew, the stink of curry in Joe's building

the child laughs as the green bird
pinches a seed from her fingers

sour tumbles with the sweet
the house is full of plastic flowers
and doilies freshly starched
outside, the garden has grown lush and shady
with potatoes, beans and lettuce
and beer-filled lids to drown the slugs

for the child a plate of sugar cookies
and a glass of lemonade

those deviants should all be thrown in jail
those welfare bums, they make me sick

clipped wings and child's fingers
skip unscathed across the checkered cloth

tender seedlings
the old ones dredge
in the muddy slurries of their luck

The Old Country

where do we come from?
the children ask the old ones
who think: that country
what's it called now?

Austro-Hungary, the Empire
Ruthenia, I think
or try Galicia

as the children search the atlas
in vain,
all gone, all gone now,
the old ones console them
with a five dollar bill
blue as an eye
the queen extracted at some point
like a mote
their first prime minister on the money now

the old ones always call him *that English*
until one of the children says
Laurier is a French name

What! the old ones cry
and all this time, we were blaming him!
they wink at each other

but nevertheless
chalk up another irrational grievance
against Quebec

Sense of Place

THE RADIO:

"Lately there has been a rash of livestock maiming
in rural Alberta.
Several horses and calves found brutally slain
are rumoured to be the work
of a Satanic cult."

THE VETERINARIAN:

"All signs indicate the attacks
have been made by coyotes."

THE RCMP:

"The public should be assured that
there is no evidence of any Satanic practices
being carried out by any individual or group of individuals
in the province of Alberta at this point in time."

NEPHEW ON THE FAMILY FARM:

"Now that Aunt Annie's in a home,
we'll tear down her shack, sell the calves,
and plant another field of GMO canola."

PROFESSOR OF CANADIAN LITERATURE:

"Surely it is the spectre of the trickster
emerging from the subconsciously assimilated
shamanic forces in the minds of rural individuals
who are, whether they know it or not, bound
to the primal mythos of the land."

Hear them?
Hear them jeering in the gullies,
moonsick in the back rows,
howling and hungover
in the promise-poisoned fields?

Red-Winged Blackbirds on Bulrushes

ruby rings, an open Spanish fan
the blackbird's jewelled wings

strike velvet lapels of the cattails
coquettes, mutton chop men

the country waltzes on decorously
flute notes, Viennese reeds and strings

feet in sludge
bodies in the grip of modern fevers

peasants come with ploughs
shouting, brandishing machetes and torches

court ladies run for the exit
their ball gowns sizzle and shrink

the country melts off the face of the map
chandeliers rain down their diamonds

peasants accept toxic treaties and oily tools
the Archduke takes a disguise and loses himself

the businessman sinks into a chair
fingers medallions, a bulbous watch

so much left to do — sign the slough over
to a withering drought

dredge and cement
the blackbirds' dear home

Second Thoughts

i.

what if your house were getting old and crowded
so you started to build a new house
but the thing just wouldn't be made?

what if the new house refused to follow the plan
and, like the child who was different,
sat down in midair, turned away
from its own blueprints
kicked holes in its foundation

each night shingles flew off the roof
like a thundercloud of bats
the house pushed the ladder into the grass
tied green love knots around the bewildered rungs

panes of glass melted in your hands
when you tried to install the windows
newly hung doors closed once
got bored, then ran away

the old house kept doing service
staying busy, stringing up webs of laundry
dusting paths
breathing women's skirts and men's jackets
in and out its painted doors
bustling orphan calves into the barn
eating a Spartan diet of coal
helping the garden deliver
clean itself up and deliver again

while the new house refused, just refused, to be finished
shuffling cards of wood and light blue holes
dillying and dallying on the chaise longue of its legend
drowsing in the hammock of wheat fields
paddling in a bubble bath of snow

the secrets of the old house
never unearthed from the cellar
no *why*s answered, no good guesses
at what you will never know:
just the past, a family,
a country squandered and someone enriched

and the new house going its separate useless way
refusing all secrets, all prosperity
as children play in its windy ribs,
unstick newborn kittens from its fibrous walls,
swing on stepless stairs
          and loot the loft for nests and bats

stick by stick, rib by rib the new house
falls to its knees
comes apart, comes unnailed
in the rain's clean fingers
until it is gutted, open-roofed, incomplete
as an unanswered prayer

ii.

I am a mother now
so I sit on the sensible steps of the old house
and I look at the ruin that was never lived in
and think, *what folly*

the wind grabs the unformed house
by the scruff of its neck
spits into a facecloth
and scrubs the nonsense off its stubborn face

such screeches, such protests!
a swirl of apron and arms
and flapping floorboards
and scolds and *let go of me*s
until suddenly they burst apart

the wind clapping her hands
the ruin released and furious
the old house humming
with approval

I lean on the steps of that sensible house
but keep hearing the child sobbing with frustration

I have to try to think both ways

so I stand up
and walk across the field
I climb the broken steps
and walk through the doorless frame

HUNTING THE SAINT

The Reliquary Speaks to Me

first, the saint's body was torn apart
and passed around like bread
bone and hair
loosened from the crust
(you called this love)

then, the yellowed stub
was given to me,
barely enamelled
(the way children were given to you)

the golden lid thudded shut beneath
the weight of jewels and fat thumbs
(the way you tried to raise them, vainly)

now, nothing disturbs me
I cannot be robbed

my hinge
is the delicate nailed mouth of God

while yours
is a wrench
undoing nothing

Her Stillborn Child

> *August 5, 1914 — I had expected that by this time I would have had my baby. But my hour is not yet come . . . I wish greatly that it was all over . . . I am full of forebodings.*
>
> — L.M. MONTGOMERY

i.

a priest has bought her kitchen
detached it from her family home and moved it,
now this small cabin
is planted by a sandy Island lake

O father who art
in Prince Edward Island
what does he feel there with her?

the warm surge of rural blood
washed with weekly transformations
the red Edwardian soil
the lapping years of menstrual cramps
the prosperous slaughter by the sea
and a single star scratching an inky sky

he's aging rapidly in the severed piece
of her first home

ii.

outside the kitchen the black snow
panics against the icy panes
she wrote in her journal
of deepening winter and
of her lover's hands in the farmhouse parlour
remembered

mother and darkling flirt
your fiancé is doom-seduced
the lick of hell is in his eye
and waits for you (you think it's you)

members of the church,
her legs are sheathed in long black stockings
she lets them watch her walking down the aisle
religious men, they always write of women

and so do we
I do. I do.
the paper fan with which she cools our girlhood
flushes open white and shuts in darkness

the lover that never never
the salvation that never never
came
the century
stepping through trenches
to reach the knot of unborn
over book over
sweet physical objects
the final hue and cry
it's over
and the remains
just gaping holes in poetry
the birthing bed empty
the earth's muscles
slit open, pouring, pouring

her breasts
white stones

iii.

the rest of her house is burnt now
the bedroom where her grandmother
slept in her abusive dreams
and the narrow pinching stairs
rushing down in flames

but a priest
a Catholic priest
has saved this room

Godly man
the black snow fills the ploughed up ground
Godly dying man
and God a man
who dealt you this
this piece of prophecy
his soft and wretched hand
must be
forgotten and to forget
this must
be gotten
down

What We Did For Mother's Day

for Doug and Jennifer

I was playing cars with my younger brother at eight
a.m. when our little sister found us and said,
"What did you get for mom, you guys?" Hoarded
dusty chocolates flashed before our ingrate
eyes, but my brother suddenly thought of the paper
thingamajig he'd made in school, squashed
by books, but presentable with tape.

But I — selfish, ungrateful eldest child —
I had to work hard, I had to create
something really good, like decorate
a card — a card! so cheap! . . . except if filled
with a poem that rhymed, gilded with unicorns
and roses, even though the pink crayon was lost.
I prayed my mother slept in. This was my forlorn

hope. My brother and sister promised not
to wake her. Thank God the house was carefully still.
Or was it? Because why had their stupid game now spilled
into the hallway outside her room? I caught
them running and giggling and bouncing off the walls!
Pigs! What if she wakes and my doggerel jewel's
immature, disfigured, my drawing partial?

Anything for that *How nice dear. Is it . . .*
ah, a . . . , yes, here's a special spot
beside my bed. The pressure to be thought
the artistic child. Those brats will make me mess it.
Oh how to find a rhyme for *rainbow* now?
Is there time to chuck that line and start anew?
Is the art to try to beat the time somehow?
Or are my glorious days of favour through?

The Decline of Irresponsibility

One warm wet winter by the sea
she will have a white wedding,
damp and ill-attended.
The slender organ pipes already vibrate.
The bride's hair and skin are moist
beneath the bodice and pale hooks.
She moves forward into satin,
her mind hot and bothered with vows.

On her honeymoon she will
walk along the sea shore
through a wealthy neighbourhood
where the arrogant lawns
claim the beach beneath her feet.

Soon, soon, the sea air will slowly force
the long white wedding dress
to unfold, to richly open.
She'll buy this thing she desires,
and that.

But in another city, she'll be a single
mother. The winter amaryllis
sold in Safeway boxes will crowd the shelves.
They will tempt her.
She can't afford them.
Her children are caged in the shopping cart.
Her government cheque is folded in her purse.
She buys twelve litres of cold milk,
and closes her eyes through the plant section.
The bouquets stiffen.
The milk wobbles in its plump bags
and the round fists of the children
cling to the metal mesh.

In the produce aisle,
she pries open their small mouths,
feeds each one of them
a stolen grape.

The Children Make Valentines on My Thirtieth Birthday

I trace paper hearts for them to cut and paste
          a Valentine heart is pointed
                    my pencil draws it sharp

and when the baby cries
          the milk is piercing

is thirty too young to stop
          with three children
                    only
          the kitchen floor is patched
                    with crooked hearts
                              chopped sheets of paper
                                        my handwriting shreds and falls
                    from their plump hands

bright noise   and generous
          with glue
                    their Valentines dent softly
          when I press them
                    whiteness oozes out the sides

the children's wet and sticky hands
                    comb paper hearts from my hair
                              my lips

                    I cannot walk away
                    without small hearts
                    sticking to my feet

and thirty crimson fingers pressing
          at my breast

Vestigial Names

Now that we use so much
ultrasound
do children have them,
those unusable, alternate
names our parents gave us
before they saw us?

Was I once a creature
with a girl name and
a boy name, possibilitied,
and double-natured,
mysteriously twinned
and two-sexed
until the wet and gory
revelation?

When I tell my sons
their girl names,
they look embarrassed. Are they
worried their girl names show?
My dears, I say,
never being born they cannot
haunt you and I will never
tell your friends.

Still, I think of them
fondly, our lost names.
How once
we played in a sea
of sound, drank
new words daily,
and in our multi-languaged
mouths rolled
our single syllables
around.

Canadian Sonnets for my Son

for Douglas

His dreams begin on the museum's fourth floor.
Luminous cases display burnished muskets,
pikes, maces, double-handed swords
longer than his body, ruby-encrusted
daggers and, mostly, empty knights in armour.
He's too young to read that the chain mail gauntlet
is Italian-made, the breastplate new, no war —
just show — for the nineteenth-century German helmet,
but he sees himself behind those slitted sights.
He's decked in tunic, scabbard; he's sacked the displays.
One day he'll go to Scotland to see the castles
and where do they live now, the steeds and knights?
Both here and there. He joins these separate places:
a myth of kings, lit glass and faded tassels.

And I start in Toronto's gallery, surprised
by Holbein's sketches. The gaze of Thomas More
fells mine. Stripped faces now have no disguise
but pencil. Hair bound back, just the pure
bones, lips, eyes. The labels recover
names: one, not a nurse of the young Prince
as formerly thought, but a great Greek scholar;
George Carewe, captain of the *Mary Rose* — since
famously dragged from the sea in silver streams;
and, mostly, Henry Howard's long calm face:
"he brought the sonnet and blank verse to England."
Outside the concrete building, our tongues steam
with English. It's winter in this foreign place
called home where we two travellers, dazzled, land.

He Loves Archaeology

the bones wait
unlike the busy parts of the body

muscles and tendons jog about from the day we are born
carry us kicking and screaming into our lives,
inside us, the needy organs are always thirsty
always complaining, always straining against their membranes,
our skin tosses and turns
even as it soothes us,
it is our slingshot in childhood
and our sagging hammock in old age

but the bones
in the midst of all this fuss and fury
are secret, introverted;
they keep their coded tablets
in rubber suitcases, padded with tissue and locks;
you can break them
but you can never make them speak

it's only when the body's sweetness is rinsed away
one cell at a time
when the battered heart picks its way
out of the ruins
when the juices of the eyes and tongue
have finally drained away

that the universal system is exposed:
and now they flaunt — those bones —
their cryptic constellation
of sticks and stones

What Is Wrong?

The psychologist says, "What is wrong with this picture?"

Two cartoon children are walking to school,
carrying books in their arms.
It takes a few seconds for you to realize
the shadows of the children are
criss-crossed.
An impossible state of physics.

You stare at your child anxiously.
Will he see the mixed-up shadows?
Will he get it?
But the child has noticed something else.
The child says, "They forgot their backpacks."

How can this be wrong?
Every morning as he leaves for school you say:
"Don't forget your backpack."
His answer can't be wrong.
Except it is.
Shadows fall in only one direction.

So this is the test that you remember.

And the first clue to the diagnosis:
maybe you are pleased
your voice is so powerful in him,
more powerful than the sun.

He Loves Islands

The boy stands at the rail of the boat
watching the island swim towards him,
first a dot, small as a seal's head,
then long and smooth as a dolphin,
and soon a whale-sized swimmer
hauling itself through the sea
to his outstretched hand.

The island stops its huge front crawl long enough
for the boy to scramble onto its muscular back.
It bobs like a boat beneath the boy.
He jumps up and down to make the island rock.
He leans over the edge of the dock
to see giant limbs paddle in the weeds.

For hours he rides the island's beachy
shoulders, watches eagle fingers reach
up to the sky and dip into the sea.
There is power and safety
on an island, forests and boulders
its mighty cargo,
cliffs careening in the wind,
and gulls looping
halos overhead.

So whenever he can,
he shows he's grateful:
he throws stones
at the water

that's always bothering,
always blocking,

the island's huge heroic stride.

A Question He Failed on the IQ Test

"Define *island,*"
the psychologist says.

The child who loves islands
has a speech
disorder. Though his room
is full of maps,
he can
barely talk.

"It's land. Land, it's . . ."

Not the right answer.
The psychologist darkens
the little black box.

"Next question. Pay attention
and listen carefully."

Tell me who is listening.
Does the test have ears?
Can the fat pencil trace
the faulty nerve
to the brain?
Is every tool too clumsy to
hear this child
longing
to tell his love?

"Land, it's land . . ."

It's Ithaca, Ireland, Iceland,
and the sea is all around,

listen,

the sea is all around.

A Test: Non-Verbal Learning Disorder

i.

delicately the skull
clamps the brain in place

and eyes moor
their light in the brain

ears dip flutes
into this funnel, that fold

and the mind polices
all harbours of thought

ii.

geometry is the mind humming
wordlessly at a task

geometry is as ancient as a palace
or even a tent

geometry walks endless corridors

it is a procession through
looms and columns
its back is broken on the lip of pottery
it lies in steel vaults and hulls of ships

and here it is again
in rows of cards
that tile the top of the table

here it is again sliding smoothly
through the psychologist's hands

iii.

the examiner will not stop to ask

does this hurt?
is there a small stone in your sandal?
why will the paths not join?

the examiner has never been lost
in the labyrinth of a triangle

yet what shape does not dizzy
the footsteps of the young hero
being tested

and failing?

the nerve of his eye has flattened
into a black sail

his ear is a corner
that bends his voice away from him

circles collapse
ovals keel over
on the page

every shape invents a new direction
to a dead end

iv.

the hero kneels on the pattern
he looks hard

the harder he looks
the more the pattern melts

into piles of loose string
that pool in the centre of his stare

when the hero is alone
he takes his skull

dips it into the black well
draws the only line he can

hauls on it, pulls up

— what will it be?

the ghastly Minotaur
slashed and bleeding?

or what?
his inner eye undone
tangled up in all the measured thread
that dropped?

He Loves the Labyrinth

At the heart of the maze there's always some cheesy grotto,
or scrawny little yew tree,
or tattooed rock.
The children always lose interest once they get there.
Instead, they want to go back to the glee of getting lost.

So, it's how to get out again.
It's how to find him when he might be panicking.
It's having to trust his older brothers to figure out the system
so the rescue team will work.

And he won't just stay in one place until you find him.
He won't let you hold his hand, all the way in
and all the way out.
He has to do it on his own.
He has to get lost all by himself.

It's having to trust the path to keep him safe.
It's having to believe he can't get lost in a circle.
It's having to believe in civilization and its designs.
It's having to stand at the mouth of the maze
staring at a hole plugged up with evergreen.

Voices saturate the shrubs and hedges,
like water in a sponge.
The leaves and twigs are mixed up
with *Where Are You*s and *Hello*s.
You want to squeeze him out.

But he won't be ordered or handed out.
Somewhere in there
he's in love with his loss.

Praying

tonight my prayer
is a chopping block

I lay a large hope upon it
as the world comes crashing down

the prayer holds the hope steady
until under the blow

it splinters into hundreds
of smaller hopes

flying off
in all directions

He Loves Mythology

i.

On TV, the concerned journalist interviews the weapons inspector. "Do you believe Iraq has weapons of mass destruction?" The inspector believes he can say, "There is no evidence that Iraq has weapons of mass destruction." The journalist shakes her CNN blonde hair, frowns, raises an excommunicating finger: "But do you believe Iraq has weapons of mass destruction? Do you *believe* it?"

ii.

In an elementary school in another city, the boy who struggles even to hold a pencil must draw a picture to illustrate his favourite book: the *Iliad,* a child's abridged version, a book he loves, a book he's read a dozen times. For him, the paper is as hard to hold onto as a stringless kite in the wind. His crayons rebel in his fingers. Still, he manages to draw two puffy warriors battling it out with balloon-like swords. When the teacher sees the picture, she tells him he has done it wrong. "You should have drawn this big wooden horse. Don't you see the picture on the cover?" Except she hasn't read the book. She doesn't know the *Iliad* is about Achilles and his battles, and not that weapon of mass destruction, the Trojan horse. Later, once the children have gone home, she does her daily devotion: "It is clear the child's reading comprehension is far below normal." Do you believe? Do you *believe* it?

St. George and the Dragon

When I finally looked into its jewelled eye,
I was mystified.
Though my spear was in its throat,
it had me.
It drank my triumph
as if the lance were a silken strap of wine
syringing into its thirsty jaws.

Now, eternally,
crackling in gold foil,
we swivel through this moment.
Over one shoulder,
I see my son writhing on a stake,
but I must turn away.
From an upper window of a castle,
a woman beckons.
Her breasts are shooting stars,
her fingers banners blowing,
but unchanged I orbit on
the axis of the weapon.

I cannot end my victory.
I am up to my elbows in hot red chains,
stapled to the deathly heart
of Glory.

Special Needs Jesus

he was the product of an uneventful pregnancy
though his mother described being under a great deal of stress
for his father had unpredictable mood swings
and periods of extreme withdrawal and significant rage

from the beginning the son needed a modified and adapted
individual education plan:
while everyone else was on holiday
he was slogging away in the temple, sitting with the doctors
trying to understand the rules, to ask the right questions

through testing it has become clear
he has severe difficulties with categorical, sequential and
analogical thinking: note his confusion as he struggles
with the five loaves and two fishes
believing he can feed the five thousand

in fact, he has an exceptionally weak fund
of practical information and common sense knowledge:
consider his observations like "Blessed are the meek
for they shall inherit the earth"
or the time he got lost in the desert
for forty days and forty nights

his cognitive disorder makes processing complex
visual-spatial material a challenge:
once he walked out into the middle of the lake
mistaking water for land, and was later unable to comprehend
his friends' concerns

which indicates another area of disability:
he often exhibits significant deficits in social judgment and
social interaction:
remember his behaviour in the bank, his choice of unreliable
friends,
his association with various lepers and losers
those which are lunatic and those which are palsied
those who cry out and cut themselves with stones

when under pressure, he demonstrates expressive language
impairment
perhaps compounded by extreme reticence and word-finding
difficulties:
simple questions like "Art thou the King of the Jews?"
are answered inappropriately with "Thou sayest"
and when the tester asks again, he answereth nothing

in every case, the mother has been supportive but ineffectual
wringing her hands, tagging along behind the experts
waiting outside doors, watching the prophecy unfold
her only consolation being that when there's no faith and
little hope,
at least there's love

and the father — well, thank God he has forsaken them

in our opinion, it is hardly surprising
this child believes the solution is to start all over
no wonder he thinks he should be born again

Effigy

At the beach, my child slowly buries me.
He packs the sand into a pail. When
It's full, he ices the damp cement smoothly
Between the pail's parted lips and then
Dumps the fragile cones on top of me.
Warm and rotten bricks, they crumble: but only
At first a dusty sheet, dry and shroudy —
Soon a suit of armour made of stone.

Buried alive, I'm now his monument.
Beneath the heavenly vault, I cannot raise
A hand or ease the vice of ribs around
My heart. As children must, he will prevent
The wrath of gods that rise. Today he plays
His future plans to keep me in the ground.

Pagans of the Bible Belt

My eldest child was on the playground
surrounded by his entire grade two class
when someone asked,
"Who *doesn't* believe in God?"
My son was the only one
who put up his hand.

My second child hated to offend anyone.
When his friends invited him to church,
he attended out of politeness
but thereafter told crazy lies
to avoid certain sleepovers
on Saturday nights.

My third son, I took to a cathedral.
He noticed the gruesome god
nailed to the cross and, at the top
of his lungs in a devoutly milling crowd,
yelled: "Who is this Jesus guy anyway?"

Finally, I admitted I had neglected
their spiritual education.
Remedial lessons began.
But from the beginning,
they were sceptics and truants.
"If he was a *real* god, the Romans
couldn't have killed him."
and
"Lots of heroes
went to the underworld, you know,
like Gilgamesh and Odysseus."

Soon the older two
were god-school drop-outs.

But my youngest child hangs on.
I think — no,
I believe — he has potential:
I'm sure he doesn't mean
those things he says.
I'm sure he's becoming a fan,
at least a little,
of the blue-skinned and elephant-headed
Hindu gods.

Michelangelo's *David* Revisited

In Europe, the only way to get the kids into an art gallery
was to send them on a saint hunt.

In the National Gallery, the Louvre, the Uffizi,
I let them loose with instructions
about saints and their symbols:

– Lucy carries her eyes in a bowl;
– Sebastian has arrows stuck in him like a porcupine;
– Jerome sits around reading to a lion;
– Barbara: tower;
– Catherine: wheel;
– and Lawrence lugs around a grill.

So off they went, galloping through galleries,
hunting the saints.

When we reached the museum with Michelangelo's *David,*
I thought this would be different. This would
convert them!
The massive, breathing, snowy glory,
the warm-veined Italian iceberg,
the head of seashell lips and curls
that nearly made me swoon when I was young
and virginal.

Follow me, my children, I began to lecture.
David — the crown of art, the pinnacle of human beauty.
Blah blah heart and soul.
Voilá!

But where were they?
Had they been lost in the crush?

No! They tore around a corner,
pushed the gaping crowds aside and cried:

"Mom! This gallery is great!
They have the best St. Lawrence.
He's not just holding his grill!
He's actually being barbequed!"

So, naturally, we turned our backs
on *David*
and went to see the fun.

The Key

for Ian

The lock of the sky will turn but not open
— ROBERT BRINGHURST

suddenly tree shadows criss-cross the yard
the equinox is here
just days ago the shade was short and sharp
the children stomped on it

now they trail their shadows
through twigs and pine needles
dragging dead grass and burrs
and thistled flies into the house

now in the twine-coloured sun the birds don't sing
they cry and scratch
and there are soft black holes in the orchard
where apples used to be

after a summer of thin sheets tossed aside
the children make nests in their blankets
for the blue bunny, the squashed dolphin, the curled tiger
and their heads

a net of sunlight and gravity
trawls us through the season
we are thrown into corners of rooms
roots grab stones in the earth and hang on

the key is turning once again
its serrated edge
saws through newly dug graves and stories
in a futile rout of field, heart and school

the future streams through
the latticed light
the children's hair and limbs
are snarled knots and weeds

the key delves and stalls
my fingers fumble to close the window
trying to block
the wind's tidal rushing through the screen

A Prayer for Another Winter

Please keep us from the wrong place at the wrong time.
Let the ice on the highway make the cars slow down
        so that even the deer can step across the road.
        But first let the deer stop.
Let the fence fuss over them so they must listen
        and find another way to go around.

Please let us make it.
Let us read stories about shipwrecks
        with our arms around each other
        in an anchor of lamplight.
Let us keep our place in the book or always
        find it open by the bed.

Please let our neglects be simple.
Let the rot stay in the small bowls on the kitchen counter
        where we can see it.
Let the daylight shrink around us like an old sweater.
Let the sun come into the room sideways if it can't come in
    straight.
        Never let the phone ring for hours in an empty house.

Please let us remember to go outside,
        though not when the poplars explode in the park.
Let us stay home then, baking and cooking.
        But when it's done, let the children
        run through fresh sparks and coals.
Let them be untouched by all but time, the wind
        and their moulding black hands.

Let us not be too late, or too lost.
Let the winter come as it must, and go when it should,
    wheeling away the dead months, one at a time,
    down its septic corridor.
Let the prayer be forgotten.
Let us, help us, make it in time.

The Children Forget My Fortieth Birthday

Why do I bother
to wait up until two in the morning?

Why do I sit in the living room
wondering what they are doing
in the basement?

Why waste time making lists
of rules that fall
off the fridge in a day?

So what if they say nothing
at breakfast.

Of course they are taller
than I am.
Of course they drive away
in their cars.
I must accept that I do not know
the names of their passengers

and that I do not know how to wake them.
But they have their own alarm clocks.
And if they do sleep away whole afternoons,
well, what's it to them
that they have trained me
to get up every morning
at six A.M.?

In fact, I should celebrate
each day that is left
before they leave,
treat each day
like a birthday

when I am given mysterious presents
I can't seem to open

and my party takes place
at a house
where I am not even thought of
let alone invited.

Peripheral Vision

At night when I'm outside, the edges of my eyes
are filled with stars, but when I turn to look,
the sky is black and empty.

When I am driving by the lake, I think I see
a bird skim across the water, but when I turn to watch,
a wall of silver blinds me.

When I am walking in the forest, a birch tree glistens
further, off the path, but when I truly see this vision,
its bark is ringed with scars.

My family's voices rustle all around me when I read,
the kettle boils, feet stamp up and down the stairs.

But when I close the book, the doorway's empty.
The lonely room is all that is around to see.

Motherhood

She is the breath blown
on the window of the bus.
The children draw circles in her life
with their warm fingers
and then they rub her out.

She is the house with fragile eyes.
Everything goes in and
out of her.
Doors slam, both coming
and going.

She is the photo album
in the bottom of the trunk in the basement,
full of pictures not needed for her to remember,
full of faces only she
will ever know.

The Future

the autumn leaf holds up its hand
in warning
turn back, turn back
the red hand
flashes in the woods

because here it comes
that second summer creeping
off the lake
to lull us with its lies

the children fall
for the glamorous guest, just arrived
with her lap of exotic presents
and woods all leaved
in Christmas ribbons

her paths rip open crimson tissue
wrapping, blue sky breaks though torn
and trampled meadows
a party until

she rises up and leaves a mess
a wreck of needles, broken twigs
exhausted hills roll onto their backs

time to come in
we call

but the children chase
the disappearing leaves

time to come home

it takes so long to clean up
we must get the children to bed
it could snow at any minute

come in, come home

but too late, too late
they've gone too far

and the forest lifts
its bristling fist

He Loves the Fog

for Alex

My little boy jumps out of the car
and runs into the cloud,
his hands open.

He is sure he can grab handfuls of wet and woolly grey
and touch and bat its thickness,

but no —
the fog parts as soon as he comes near;
his heat and colour burn a clearing.
The cloud withdraws.
No matter where he turns,
his hands stay empty.

He can't shake
his small circle of clarity.
He cannot gather into his arms
the heavy pelt of fog, its fat animal body.

He must be bewildered.
I think he slows.
I'm sure he stops.

He doesn't know
that when he looks
back

(wherever you are
don't look,
don't look back, Alex)

I'll be gone.

Moon

for all three of you when you were little

In the backseat, the child, twisting about, suspects it first.
"I think the moon is following us."
We look, and sure enough,
like an eager young horse that comes to the fence

it's at our window, walking alongside
with a graceful, tugging stride
then trotting as we turn onto the highway,
and, as we speed up, cantering, first on one side of the car

and then the other, swerving in front of us,
behind us, now galloping over the lake leaving a silver gash,
running smack into a patch of cloud,
throwing black and white dust in our eyes,

busting over the hill and once
gone so long, we grow quiet and worried.

But no! It's back, loping down a mountain slope.

In time, we pull into the driveway, fling open our doors,
hands outstretched, welcoming the moon home!
But the moon backs off, salty-sided, its wild blue eyes
ranging over the star-barbed meadows.

Slowly it leaves, makes its own way through the dark.

ABOUT THE AUTHOR

NANCY HOLMES has published three other collections of poetry, *Valancy and the New World* (Kalamalka Press), *Down to the Golden Chersonese: Victorian Lady Travellers* (Sono Nis) and *The Adultery Poems* (Ronsdale). Her poetry and fiction have been published in dozens of journals and in several anthologies across the country. She was born in Edmonton, Alberta, went to high school in Toronto and university in Calgary where she received her MA in English. She has lived in the Okanagan valley of British Columbia for the past fourteen years and teaches Creative Writing at the University of British Columbia Okanagan. She is the mother of three nearly grown-up sons and lives with her family in Summerland, B.C.